International Taxation in Nepal

Tips to foreign investors

Bhava Nath Dahal

Copyright © 2018 Bhava Nath Dahal

All rights reserved.

ISBN: 9781729207673

DEDICATION

Dāsu Bhātta, Shivāram Pādhyā, Bashudev Pādhyā, Benumadhāv Pādhyā,

Tulāram Pādhyā, Shankār Pādhyā, Kāshināth, Hirāmani, Govindā,

Gobardhān, Umāpati, Srināth, Govindānath,

Bhimnāth – Kāusalyā

CONTENTS

CORPORATE REQUIREMENTS 1

PERMANENT ESTABLISHMENT 7

TAX REGISTRATION AND DEREGISTRATION 16

TRANSFER PRICING RULE 19

CORPORATE TAX 25

WITHHOLDING TAX 35

CAPITAL GAIN TAX 40

DIVIDEND TAX AND REPATRIATION TAX 44

TAX DEADLINES 47

TAX SPARING BENEFIT 51

FORECE OF ATTRACTION RULE 56

CHANGE IN CONTROL 59

VALUE ADDED TAX 62

TAX ADMINISTRATION 67

WORD INDEX 71

FORWORDS

Taxation is one of the major factor for financial decision. For a transitional economy, foreign investment is one of the major attraction for their sustainable development and modernization of the traditional economy. To switch into liberalized open economy and boost modern economy, they need foreign investments and foreign business enterprises. Foreign investors, in other hand, need deeper information on the business environment from the transitional countries. Because of absence of enough foreign investors and existence of foreign chain of experts, the foreign investors face the difficulties to obtain appropriate information from those countries.

My experience reads the information flow to the foreign investors is cumbersome process. To obtain a little of knowledge on taxation or for initial information regarding Nepal tax, foreign investors, firstly contact their domestic tax expert and latter finds 'someone' in Nepal having knowledge on taxation. To find that someone, they need to search a long chain of contact within their own network. Their contacted person may or may not be a tax expert. Almost cases, information need to that investor is exceptionally basic information or a gentle basic information. Ultimately, the potential investor pays a sizable sum to obtain vary basic information.

This is the collection on the international aspect of Nepal taxation to cover those basic need of foreign investors without the support from long-chain of information flow. Any suggestion in this regards is highly appreciable.

Bhava Nath Dahal
Kathmandu, Nepal
October 31, 2018

ACRONYMS

AISR	Anti-Income Splitting Rule
BOOT	Built, Own, Operate and Transfer
DOI	Department Of Industry
DTAs	Double Taxation Avoidance agreements
FDI	Foreign Direct Investments
FoA	Force of Attraction
GAAR	General Anti-Avoidance Rule
IBN	Investments Board of Nepal
JV	Joint Venture
NPR	Nepali Rupee
OCR	Office of the Company Registrar
OECD	Organisation for Economic Cooperation and Development
PAN	Permanent Account Number
PE	Permanent Establishment
TCS	Tax Collected at Source
UN	United Nations
VAT	Value Added Tax
WHT	Withholding Tax

CORPORATE REQUIREMENTS

01 **May a foreign entity have business set up in Nepal?**

Yes, a foreign entity may have business set up in Nepal in almost all of the business industry except a few negative list industries. The corporate form of business may be either subsidiary or branch or similar structure. However, the representative or a liaison office cannot enter into a business activities according to provisions of corporate law. Few cases of subsidiary working in service sector, controlling shareholders must be resident of Nepal.

For practical reasons and differences in various regulators, few cases like hydropower project, a subsidiary is a requirement over a branch or similar set up. In the other cases, a branch or similar set up is sufficient for Nepal business.

02 **What is the timeline for forming a liaison office, representative office, branch or a subsidiary?**

It depends upon the three factors of the business. Firstly, the line of business, whether there is requirement of license for that business or not. Secondly, the approval channel for the foreign direct investments (FDI). Thirdly, the regulatory approval, if the business requires that.

CORPORATE REQUIREMENTS

Registration of a liaison office has only two requirements – permission from Department of Industry (DOI) and registration with Office of the Company Registrar (OCR). In case the applicant fulfills all the documentary requirements, permission from DOI takes few days and OCR takes just one or two days.

Registration of a branch office has similar requirements as a liaison office. In this case, permission from Department of Industry (DOI) takes more time than a liaison office.

There are two channels for approval of foreign investments – small and medium size foreign investments through Single-window procedure of Department of Industry (DOI) and large investments through Investments Board of Nepal (IBN). Once a foreign investor obtains license and letter of intent from either DOI or IBN, it can open a subsidiary.

Opening a subsidiary or branch those requiring license takes a sizable time to obtain license from concern department.

In all above cases, the corporate set up requires to obtained permission for FDI from central bank and require to register in Permanent Account Number of taxation authority. Both cases, it takes just a day, if all documentary requirements submitted well along with application.

03 **Are there special corporate governance requirements like total number of shareholders, directors, local resident director or local agent?**

Nepal corporate law permits single shareholder private company. Maximum shareholders in a private company or minimum shareholders in a public company has fixed by corporate law. Minimum A subsidiary of a public company is a public company. The number of minimum director in a public company is fixed in corporate law. In some business line like in banking, independent director (other than shareholders) is a requirement. In that case, local resident director appears, otherwise, subsidiary of a foreign company need not appoint local resident in its director.

Foreign supplier or contractor bidding under public procurement laws, needs a local agent for its administrative assistance. However, a branch or a subsidiary need not any agent from resident local.

04 Does Nepal business set up requires domestic documentation?

Either cases of foreign branch or subsidiary or liaison office, requires to maintain sufficient documentation regarding its corporate decisions, financial transactions and foreign exchange transaction. They need to prepare books of accounts (language either in Nepali or in English). The books of accounts have to be audited by a person having certificate of practice on auditing.

The documents those are not in Nepali or English need to be translated into Nepali on the cost of respective person. In the practice, translation into English is accepted.

Each type of form of set up requires to file their corporate returns to OCR and tax return (even zero-return) to the taxation authority.

The documents relating to a transaction must retain for six years from end of concern fiscal year.

05 Does Nepal have any other basic regulatory issues?

Foreign branch or subsidiary need to permission and requires to file details for any inwards foreign investments in either form of equity or borrowings. Similar permission and approval requires to repatriate repayments. Both processes are simple in easy-fashion. For importation of goods or services, permission for use of foreign currency is a requirement.

Importing a new technology is welcomed but permission from DOI is required to pay the cost for import.

Subsidiary company requires to file its periodic returns with OCR disclosing annual general meeting, extra-ordinary general meeting, appointment of auditors and other prescribed information.

CORPORATE REQUIREMENTS

Nepal fiscal year or a tax-year is based on Nepali calendar, which starts somewhat mid-July and end on next mid-July. All the recordings require to follow Nepali calendar for the accounting, reporting, and filing any return. For a monthly return, only Nepali calendar month is permissible, which almost mid-month to mid-month basis. Foreign business person must aware of these calendar system to avoid the penalties or fees for non-compliance.

Recording or reporting currency is Nepali Rupees (NPR). Person wishing to record their transactions in currency other than NPR, need to use dual currency books of accounts or reports.

Official language is Nepali for all correspondence or dialogue. Practically, English is accepted in almost all cases, except for prescribed formats. Many legal formats are available in English too.

Governmental working hours is 10:00 to 5:00 pm from Sunday to Friday. Online portals, if they have, accept day-end at mid-night. Almost private agencies follow same pattern of governmental working hours and days. Few of the business wings related to multi-national institutions follows five-days from Monday to Friday.

Nepal emphasizes equal-opportunity employments. Few cases, there is governmental incentive to the private employer based on proportion of female or incapacitated persons.

06 **Does Nepal has rule of privacy? Do the government agencies disclose the commercial information they collected during their official duty?**

Information filed with OCR are, legally, public documents. Therefore, OCR collects only the corporate information on structure of shares, basic information of shareholders or directors, but not the personal information of shareholders and directors.

Banks requires to follow strict rule of secrecy of its customers. Bank itself may use that information for banking purpose only. Information submitted to the banks are secret for private use.

Information submitted to taxation authority are secret. The authority itself can use for taxation purpose only. Based on the tax treaty, it may share the information to the competent authority of contracting state during exchange of information.

Auditor General have almost full excess on the information obtained by various agencies. However, information collected during the audit cannot be disclosed elsewhere.

Courts are open courts, but the filing of case is possible by a taxpayer only. Information submitted to the court or discussion within the court procedure are open to public.

Taxation authority may create the charge on assets and properties registering letter to various agencies in the case of non-payment of tax arrears. During the auction to recover tax arrears, minimum information those requires to make a public auction will be disclosed. But, in none case, business information of any taxpayer cannot be disclosed.

There are few legal channels, where more than one governmental agencies may exchange the information with limited purpose as prescribed by the law itself.

None of the agency may seek any information regarding technical or commercial formula, secret formula, know-how or technological design.

07 How does tax residency determine for taxation?

Any of three residency criteria makes an individual as tax resident – normal domicile, stay of 183-days in a tax-year or governmental employees.

Entity incorporated in Nepal is resident for tax purpose. For this case, place of effective management and affairs is immaterial. For the entity, which has not incorporated in Nepal, i.e. incorporated outside Nepal or unincorporated elsewhere, it will be resident for tax if there is effective place of management in Nepal in whole or in part during the year.

CORPORATE REQUIREMENTS

08 **Does foreign investor need to disclose the sources of income to make Nepal investments?**

Nepal has anti-money laundering law. Investors need to disclose and declare the source of income and its legitimacy. In bank deposit more than NPR 1 million (roughly US$ 10,000), they need to disclose the fact of source. For borrowed fund or capital injection through banking channel, just the approval of foreign direct investments from approving authority is enough.

For the investments made before mid-April 2019 for infrastructural business and manufacturing business having more than three hundred employees consuming domestic raw materials more than 50% of total raw material, even the declaration of source is not compulsory.

PERMANENT ESTABLISHMENT

09 **Does Nepal tax have concept of permanent establishment (PE)?**

Nepal tax law has concept of permanent establishment. According to tax law, "Permanent Establishment" means a place from where a person fully or partially conducts business; the term includes the following places:

(1) A place where a person fully or partially conducts business through an agent, other than a general agent who functions in an independent manner, in the ordinary course of conducting business. [dependent agent]

(2) A place where the main equipment or the main machinery of a person is kept, used, or installed. [fixed-base]

(3) One or more places of a country where a person has provided any technical, professional, or consultancy service through employees or otherwise for more than ninety-days in any period of twelve-months, [presence for service]

(4) A place where a person is engaged in a construction, assembly, or establishment project for ninety-days or more in any period of twelve-months, and the place from where the supervision activities of the project are conducted. [construction site]

PERMANENT ESTABLISHMENT

10 **Can an employee or an employee from other foreign subsidiary (or other type of associated person) or use of domestic sub-contractor or use of foreign sub-contractor create a PE?**

A domestic agent except independent in nature, a fixed base, a construction site or a service in Nepal is a PE for Nepal tax. Business of individual is not a PE; it is taxed as an individual. PE is a resident entity for Nepal tax purpose. Definition of PE, above, is purely based on 'place' not on revenue creation. For service, it is based on revenue creation as well as place. Nepal business of foreign entity through either own employee, employees from other subsidiary or associated person, Nepal sub-contractors or through foreign sub-contractors triggers a PE. Of course, there is minimum time ceiling for a site-PE or service-PE.

Nepal business through foreign sub-contractors (from own group or independent sub-contractor), depending upon the presence in Nepal or nature of business, may create further PE to sub-contractor itself. For example, Japan Inc. has construction site in Nepal, however sub-contracted to a Malaysian subsidiary. In this case, Japan Inc. has PE in Nepal based on construction site and Malaysian subsidiary has also PE based on actual construction site. Furthermore, if India subsidiary takes supervisory activity on that site, then it will be third PE, if its presence in Nepal more than 183 or more days based on Nepal-India DTA.

11 **Is there different timeframe creating a PE for resident from tax-treaty country?**

Site-PE and service-PE, two conditions for creating a PE has time-frame threshold. For a site-PE, it is ninety-days or more and for a service-PE, it is more than ninety-days in any twelve-months period. Remaining two conditions of fixed-place of business or business through dependent agent has not any time threshold. Based on respective DTA, PE from resident of either Austria, China (mainland), India (site-PE only), Republic of Korea, Mauritius, Norway, Pakistan, Qatar and Thailand, the period is 183-days instead of ninety-days. For Site-PE of Sri Lanka and service–PE from resident of India and Sri Lanka, the period remains ninety-days only.

12 How does Nepal tax determine the agency is a dependent agency?

Tax law itself has not described the eligibility of or criteria for dependent agent. Nepal has Agent law to register an agent. Even, agent law is also silence on technicality for dependent or independent agent is we discuss on taxation.

Practically as well as based on the DTAs where Nepal is a contracting state, the business in Nepal owned by a foreign from the resident in Nepal is a dependent agent. It covers, at least, any one of following rights or activities from agent on behalf on foreign principal towards:

i. authority to negotiation of business contracts;

ii. not having authority, but habitually exercised to negotiate contract;

iii. authority to conclude contract;

iv. not having authority, but habitually exercised to conclude contract;

v. expressively or habitually maintain the stock of goods for sale;

vi. expressively or habitually secures orders for the principal and other enterprises which are controlled by it or have a controlling interest in it.

13 How does taxable profit from a PE determine? Is there force of attraction rule?

According to Nepal tax law, PE is a resident entity. Business profits of a PE is determined based on separate-entity concept, which is similar to determination of taxable profit of a domestic resident company. all the business incomes are inclusions for taxable profits. All the expenses to earn those business profits are deductible expense. For deductions, it must fulfill the prescribed compliance procedure. The minimum compliance procedures are:

i. Earning rule – only expense made for earning taxable profit is deductible.

ii. Tax-period rule - expensed within tax-year is deductible (means, no prior-years, no pre-paid).

PERMANENT ESTABLISHMENT

iii. Billing rule – only the expense whose supporting evidences on the name of taxpayer is deductible.

iv. Banking process – only the expense paid through banking procedure (if more than Rupees fifty thousand) is deductible.

v. Negative items – expense for a penalty on breach of law or distribution to beneficiaries is not deductible.

Based on transfer-pricing rules (see Transfer-pricing rules on page 19 for more detail), the transaction between PE and its parent or associated enterprises of parent company is evaluated on arm's length price principle.

In few cases, force of attraction rule (see Force of attraction on page 56 in detail) apply for determination of taxable profit of a PE.

Taxpayer requires to file annual tax returns under self-assessment procedure. Taxation authority may examine the filed return within four-years. PE requires to retain all the documents relating to income or deductions or tax computation until end of five years from end of respective tax-year (for VAT, document retention period is six-years). Taxation authority may seek the documentary evidences for establishment of income, deduction and computations. In case of tax-fraud, there is unlimited reassessment period.

14 **Which triggers for a PE in case a company charging for the services will be different from the company(ies) actually carrying out the service activity? How would this pattern of facts be analyzed under Nepal tax law for PE(s) or for source rules?**

Invoicing from one person for the activities from other person(s) has not addressed in the Nepal tax law. However, any payment to third-party than actual service provider is an offence as per foreign exchange control laws. In the result, it is a criminal activity and expense for criminal activities is neither deductible for tax nor permissible for repatriate.

However, actual service provider i.e. billing company may hire their staff from anywhere with the full-responsibility. In this scenario, service-provider hires someone as sub-contractor for Nepal assignment. The company which provide services as well as the company who has legal possession on the service, both are PE if they crossed the threshold for PE.

For example, a Hong Kong company entered into service contract with Nepal company. Hong Kong company may complete the service sending its own employee or may hire anyone from elsewhere. If a staff in China company (may or may not be an associated enterprise of Hong Kong company) provides the service for Nepal, Hong Kong company may charge the bill to Nepal PE. If the presence of China staff is more than ninety-days, Hong Kong company would have a Service-PE in Nepal. Due to Nepal-China DTA, China company would not have PE in Nepal, being its presence is less than 183-days. In case, the service in Nepal was for 200-days, both Hong Kong company and China company would have Nepal PE having source in Nepal.

15 Is the business income without a PE is taxable in Nepal?

According to Nepal tax law, most of the investment payments and some of the business payments are subject to withholding tax. Therefore, in case, the payments relating to a non-resident person without having a PE in Nepal, it may attract withholding tax (see Withholding tax on page 35 in more detail). Withholding tax on payments to a non-resident is final in nature.

16 Would different entity form like PE, subsidiary, or any other form of business provide a more favorable tax result than others?

Each form of business set up has pros and cons in legal framework as well as practical parlance. Let's make a comparative analysis on subsidiary, a branch i.e. PE and a liaison office i.e. representing office with corporate law and tax law basis.

For registration of a subsidiary or a branch (PE) or a liaison office is somewhat similar. Both subsidiary or branch may involve in business activities but a liaison office (representative office) cannot.

PERMANENT ESTABLISHMENT

From the corporate law prospective, deregistration of a company is comparably difficult, practically even more than legal aspect. Deregistration of a PE is comparably easy. Disposing shares in subsidiary is easy mechanism for exit. Therefore, entry in both business model is similar; but, exit may have not similar.

For tax law prospective, registration of subsidiary as well as a PE has same level of efforts. Similar the case of deregistration. However, deregistration is possible upon payment of all tax. The person having tax disputes pending on the revenue tribunal cannot obtain the deregistration.

Transfer pricing rule is applicable to both of subsidiary and PE at same level on the transaction with associated enterprises.

In few cases of double tax avoidance agreements (DTAs), there is force of attraction rule (see Force of attraction rule on page 56 in more detail) for a PE on the same of similar business from head-office/associated enterprises. Force of attraction rule is not applicable to a subsidiary. In this case, foreign parent has favorable situation for force of attraction.

Corporate tax on similar business is same rate for subsidiary as well as for a PE. There is dividend tax at 5% of distributed amount in case of dividend from subsidiary. Similar 5% is levied on repatriation of income from a PE. Therefore, both subsidiary or PE have similar tax implication.

In brief, the most appropriate operational model to be utilized in from business, transfer pricing and tax perspectives depends upon the exact scenario of the taxpayer's presence in Nepal business. No one can say the most appropriate one without sufficient information relating to current business or prospective plan of business.

17 **Does technical service from parent company or associated enterprise to subsidiary triggers as a Nepal PE?**

Sometimes Nepal subsidiary obtains continuous services from its parent company or any of its associated enterprise may cross the time threshold of ninety-days. In this situation, domestic company, the subsidiary is resident entity for Nepal tax purpose. There is virtual PE as service-PE for its parent company due to service for more than threshold time. Additionally, each of associated enterprise, if crossed the threshold time, is separate service-PE for Nepal tax purpose.

In case of technical service from parent or associated enterprise is in form of royalty or license fee without any presence in Nepal, the technical fee itself does not trigger as a PE.

18 **Does a liaison office or representative office triggers as a Nepal PE?**

Based on Nepal corporate law, liaison office or representative office cannot involve in business activities in Nepal.

Based on international practice, a liaison office may only be a point of contact in the country. It would have almost no revenue creation in the host country. The cost of liaison office is directly chargeable to its head-office. Most cases, they do not maintain the books of accounts in the host country too. They are mainly focus on, collecting business information, advertising, display or have storage of goods only.

However, different regulating agencies in Nepal has different requirements. Harmonization on those requirements are under progress. For a liaison office, opening bank account, central bank directives instructed the commercial bank to obtain Permanent Account Number (PAN). On the other hand, PAN is a business registration for taxation purpose too. Therefore, practically, liaison office in Nepal is a PE.

19 **How does joint venture tax in Nepal? Does joint venture with two or more foreign companies tax as two separate PEs? What will be the position in case joint venture, if one of the partner of joint venture is Nepal company?**

For Nepal tax purpose, joint venture is company and not a fiscally transparent structure. Joint venture will obtain its own PAN for taxation. Same as the corporate company, JV requires to issue the invoices on JV's name, purchases on

PERMANENT ESTABLISHMENT

JV's name and requires to keep separate set of books of accounts. The accounting as well as filing tax return is similar as a registered company. The books of accounts and JV's tax return is compulsory.

Being a tax company working in Nepal, it is resident. Corporate tax is levied on taxable profit of JV. Distribution of profit among JV partners will be treated as dividend from 'company' and attracts dividend tax.

Since JV is equivalent to company for tax purpose, it is not a PE for its partners, rather they are equivalent to shareholders (beneficiaries) of the company. Therefore, JV having foreign partners or domestic partners have no-difference for Nepal tax.

20 **Does Nepal set up under chain-of-subsidiary (e.g. Hong Kong- Malaysia – Nepal or Hong Kong- Malaysia – Mauritius – Nepal) is beneficial to foreign investor?**

Nepal tax law recognize the domestic PE or domestic subsidiary as a resident entity. In all cases, the tax implication like registration, filing returns, payments of tax, dividend tax, repatriation tax etc. is same. In case of conduit entity, Nepal tax law does not permit to allow treaty benefits too. Therefore, any chain-of-subsidiary does not implicate any tax differences in Nepal. If an entity in Hong Kong wants to establish a branch for Nepal business, the tax impact is same to that direct branch (as PE) or branch through either Malaysia or further through Mauritius.

In the contract, multiple chain may create additional tax in case of change in control (see Change in control on page 62 for more detail) in foreign parent at any higher level.

21 **Taiwan-based company (Taiwan-HO) wants establishment of a subsidiary in Hong Kong (HK-subsidiary), either wholly-owned or substantially-owned. Hong Kong-based company wants investment in Nepal business through subsidiary in Nepal (Nepal-subsidiary). Nepal-subsidiary may have either wholly-owned investments company having further subsidiary**

in business company with controlling majority or substantially owned business company with minority Nepali investors. Which model is most favorable for Nepal tax prospective?

In this chain of companies, there may be four different options as:

Option 1 is, Taiwan (HO) –Hong Kong subsidiary (100%) – Nepal subsidiary business co. (>50%)

Option 2 is, Taiwan (HO) –Hong Kong subsidiary (>50%) – Nepal subsidiary business co. (>50%)

Option 3 is, Taiwan (HO) –Hong Kong subsidiary (100%) – Nepal subsidiary Investments Co. (100%) - Nepal subsidiary business co. (>50%)

Option 4 is, Taiwan (HO) –Hong Kong subsidiary (>50%) – Nepal subsidiary Investments Co. (100%) - Nepal subsidiary business co. (>50%).

All of the four option has similar tax implication based on Nepal tax law. Structural differences within control has not differentiated for either of corporate tax, dividend tax, transfer pricing or otherwise.

TAX REGISTRATION AND DEREGISTRATION

22 What is the process for a branch registration from a foreign company?

Registering a foreign branch starts from application process. Under Sec.155 (1) of Company Act, 2063 a registration application should be made to OCR along with permission (if required) from the concerned body pursuant to the prevailing law and corporate documents relating to incorporation in home country. Where any foreign company is selected by any competent body pursuant to the prevailing law or enters into contract with any competent body, for any business in Nepal, the making of such selection or entering into such contract itself is considered as the permission given by the concerned body.

Prescribed fees for application is varying with amount of capital. As an indicative, application fee at Present, is NPR 15,000 minimum for declared amount of Investment up to NPR 10 million.

Local content requirements in the application is required, which includes physical address in Nepal, authorized representative, (a foreign national can be appointed as authorized representative provided his local contact address of Nepal is recoded for such purpose).

Timing for registration with OCR is completed, normally, within a period of one week to the maximum period of thirty days, provided that all the required documents are submitted.

23 **What are the requirements for tax registration in Nepal? How long it takes to obtain registration?**

Any person having business income (except obtaining final withholding taxed income only) requires to register in Permanent Account Number (PAN) with the taxation authority before obtaining any business income. The application requires to lodge on prescribed format (now online form).

For the business attracting value added tax (VAT), it is required to apply for VAT within thirty-days from crossing of prescribed threshold. Now in 2018, prescribed threshold for VAT is transaction of goods more than Rs. 5 million, services Rs. 2 million or imports Rs. 10 thousand. Person register in VAT obtains input tax credit on capital expenditure too. Therefore, it is favorable to obtain VAT registration before any threshold consideration to obtain input tax on early investments too.

For the business attracting excise duty, it is required to apply for excise permissions before starting the business.

According to legal provision, time-span for registration is thirty-days from date of apply. However, practically it is single day work if applicant filed the documents as prescribed in application form.

Apart from federal tax registration, a person requires to register its business in respective local authorities too. However, their registration is easy as well as they levy a presumptive tax in a minor scale only.

24 **What are the minimum compliance requirements after registration?**

There are few compliance requirements, failure attract fees and penalties. At the minimum, a registered person requires to:

TAX REGISTRATION AND DEREGISTRATION

i. Display its registration certificate in the main business place (practically copy of certificate is acceptable).

ii. Display a tax-plate (10cm×30cm) in the main business place.

iii. Use PAN for the tax related documents and bank loan application, if any.

iv. Maintain the books of accounts and supporting thereto.

v. File monthly withholding tax return and monthly VAT return, if registered in VAT.

vi. File estimated tax return within six-months of tax-year.

vii. Pay installment tax on three installments (six-months, nine-months and twelve-months).

viii. File annual tax return within three months from end of tax-year, extendable further three months.

ix. Submit the information as seek from taxation authority.

25 **What are the requirements for tax de-registration in Nepal? How long it takes to de-registration?**

In case, a person closing down its business in Nepal, may apply for de-registration from taxation through prescribed format (now online form). Within fifteen-days from date of application, taxpayer requires to submit the documents as noticed by the taxation authority.

In case, there is pending tax dispute, either taxpayer waits for finalizing the issue or requires to withdraw for deregistration. Taxpayer must pay all the dues of tax arrears including the tax on the disputes pending on the taxation tribunal.

Tax officer examines the books for any discrepancy of filed tax returns. At the clearance for all respect, tax officer decides for the deregistration.

Legally prescribed time-frame for deregistration is three-months from date of application. Practically, it depends upon the settlement of disputes and arrears.

TRANSFER PRICING RULE

26 **Does Nepal has transfer pricing rules? What are the main coverage?**

In the case of transaction between associated person, they must be same value as if it was between two unrelated parties in the same scenario and conditions. For this Nepal tax prescribes for a transfer pricing rule.

For the transfer pricing, first of all, definition of associated person is critical. Nepal tax law defines an associated person as:

"Associated Person" means one or more persons working according to the intentions of another Person or a group of such persons; the term includes the following persons:

(1) A natural person and relatives or a partner.

(2) A foreign permanent establishment, and the person having ownership in that establishment, and

(3) An entity that controls or derives benefit from fifty-percent or more of the income, capital, or voting rights of another entity either by itself or in association with any person connected with it, or with an associate entity or any person or entity connected with such an associate entity."

TRANSFER PRICING RULE

Furthermore, it excludes the employees and a person prescribed by the Department as not being associated person from definition of associated person.

DTAs concluded by Nepal has some different definition of associated enterprise. Almost them are similar, reproducing here as DTA with China (Article 9 Para.1) as:

"1. Where:

a) an enterprise of a Contracting State participates directly or indirectly in the management, control or capital of an enterprise of the other Contracting State, or

b) the same persons participate directly or indirectly in the management, control or capital of an enterprise of a Contracting State and an enterprise of the other Contracting State, and in either case conditions are made or imposed between the two enterprises in their commercial or financial relations which differ from those which would be made between independent enterprises, then any profits which would, but for those conditions, have accrued to one of the enterprises, but, by reason of those conditions, have not so accrued, may be included in the profits of that enterprise and taxed accordingly."

In the tax treaties, Nepal accepted the control in management is testing measure for associated enterprises, but not much clear in domestic law.

Transfer pricing provision of the tax law states as:

"Transfer Pricing and other arrangements amongst Associates: (1) In case any arrangement has been made between persons who are associated persons, the Department may, by notice in writing, distribute, apportion, or allocate amounts to be included or deducted in calculating income between the persons as is necessary to reflect the taxable income or tax payable that would have arisen for them if the arrangement had been conducted at arm's length."

For this, taxation authority may re-characterize the source and type of any income, loss, amount, or payment, or allocate costs, including head office expenses, incurred by a person in conducting a business to the associates based on the comparative turnovers of the business, in case such costs have benefitted the associated person or persons."

The major coverage for transfer pricing rule is "that would have arisen for them if the arrangement had been conducted at arm's length".

27 **How does transfer pricing rule apply to royalty or technical fee?**

Most cases of royalty or technical fee are under permission from or registration with or based on agreement from Department of Industries(DOI). DOI permits the ratio of royalty or technical fee based on data appropriate to their decision. If the royalty or technical fees has set within the criteria agreed from DOI, then it will not attract transfer pricing rules. This rate is somewhat similar as advance pricing agreement with Inland Revenue Department.

28 **What are methods for finding arm's length price for a transfer pricing issue?**

The tax law has not prescribed any method for evaluation of arm's length price. the taxpayer may apply for advance pricing agreement in case of transaction between associated person. However, this is not mandatory nor well practiced. The act or regulation or directives has not spelt a word on pricing methods. Therefore, it is almost discretionary to taxation authority to fix a price in individual case.

29 **Does the authority accept safe-harbor rule for transfer pricing?**

The tax law has not prescribed the terminology for 'safe-harbor rule'. However, taxpayer may apply for the advance pricing agreement (APA) with the taxation authority. Period for APA will be for five-years. Within APA, the safe-harbor rule or similar mechanism is a negotiation tool to both parties.

TRANSFER PRICING RULE

30 **What are the documentation requirement in the transaction with associate enterprises? Are there transactions between associated enterprises in the group creating the need for intercompany legal agreements and transfer pricing considerations?**

Nepal tax law says the valuation will be on arm's length price and follows the separate entity concept. Based on legal text and official clarification, one cannot say the minimum documentation.

Based on main impression of 'arm's length price' and 'separate entity concept', following are the minimum documentations for transfer pricing:

i. Commercial agreements similar with terms and conditions with third parties, even legally binding in nature.

ii. Commercial invoices with due trade names.

iii. Transport and customs documents, if requires so.

iv. Banking documents, if requires.

31 **Does the transfer pricing officer verify transaction, its condition of contract or pricing thereon? Is there time-frame for verification, so that any adjustments are possible to accommodate with annual tax return?**

Taxation authority has not special section to care transfer pricing issues. Any assessment (except jeopardy assessment) from taxation authority will not be completed during the tax-year. So, that the differences, if any, may not be accommodated in the annual tax return.

Transfer pricing or whatever verification will be a part of regular reassessment by tax officer within four-years from due date of filing the tax return. Any differences through transfer pricing, if established by tax officer, the taxpayer cannot adjust with the annual tax. However, need to pay corporate tax on that difference, 100% of tax as fees for misinformation and interest at the rate of 15% p.a. till the date of payment after reassessment.

Furthermore, the payment to associated person would be deemed dividend. So, dividend tax will attract of the portion that has disallowed based on transfer pricing.

32. **Without valuation mechanism or legal backup, how does the re-characterization will establish?**

It may have two different approaches. The first, taxation authority may use some internationally accepted pricing module as comparable uncontrolled price method, resale price method, cost plus method, profit split method, transactional net margin method or most appropriate among these or other one.

The second, taxpayer aware of lack of evidences of price base on any of above method and may file the law suit against the reassessment. Authority is aware on it, so, they use the wording of 'in the same or similar case' or equivalent to it. Before enactment of full self-assessment in 2002, there was similar assessment procedure using 'in the same or similar case' even for the first assessment. The wordings 'in the same or similar case' dilutes any further evidences during judicial courses.

33. **Does Nepal tax law have general anti-avoidance rule?**

Apart from transfer-pricing rules, Nepal tax law has two additional anti-avoidance measure having equal or higher strength than transfer pricing rule. The first one is Anti-Income Splitting Rule (AISR) and the second is General Anti-Avoidance Rule (GAAR).

In case, a taxpayer arranges the streams of income such a way that the its tax liability reduces due to splitting arrangement with other party, taxation authority re-characterize the transaction. Under this scenario, there may be arrangement for deferral on tax or purely income splitting. Same treatment will apply for both cases.

Under GAAR, taxation authority looks through the substance of transaction. In case a taxpayer pays tax complied with technical requirement of tax law in formal

TRANSFER PRICING RULE

way, but in substance, with tax avoidance (or tax deferral) intention, taxation authority re-characterize the transaction to bring the tax liability at appropriate base. Legal formality and fulfillment of technical aspect of transaction in this regard will not be safeguard to the taxpayer.

CORPORATE TAX

34   How does corporate tax determine in case of a subsidiary or for a PE?

In both cases, the determination of tax profit is similar. Income are recognized near to similar as from generally accepted accounting principles. Nepal has Nepal Financial Reporting Standards compatible to International Financial Reporting Standards. Few cases, income recognizes based on special anti-avoidance rules of tax law, though they are practically limited.

For deduction of expense, few special anti-avoidance rules require to comply with real cases. Any business unrelated expense is not allowed for deduction. Provision expense is not deductible expense. The deduction need to match with business income, tax-year as well as the supporting invoices must be named on the taxpayers. Cash payment is not allowed for deduction and have long list of exception too. In all cases, penalties and fines on breach of law is not allowed.

For interest from non-resident shareholders, deductible ceiling is 50% of taxable profit before any interest income or expense. Remaining interest is allowed to carry next year. Depreciation is pool-based with rate of 5% for structural properties, 25% for furniture, office equipment and computers, 20% of vehicles and 15% for plant and machinery or other tangible assets.

CORPORATE TAX

One-third of these rate is allowed for manufacturing industry (except negative-externalities), infrastructure business, power producers, power-transmission business or BOOT. Replacement of equipment under BOOT and power business obtains terminal depreciation on the replaced out assets. Straight-line method is allowed for intangibles. Repairs and improvement cost for depreciable assets is allowed to the extent of 7% of depreciation base. Remaining amount will capitalize on respective pool of asset.

Income as recognized above less the allowed deduction will be taxable profit for Nepal tax.

In case the resident person has source of income more than one country, above calculation of income and deduction need to make on per-country basis.

Corporate tax is levied on taxable profit at the rate prescribed for the respective tax year.

The default corporate tax rate is 25% of taxable profit. Some of the business have double dividend rate of 30%, whereas many industries have reduced tax rate of 20%. Infrastructural business or power sector or BOOT obtains further concession either in corporate rate of tax or in periodic concession.

35 **What is the source rule for income or expense?**

Determination of source of income has based on two rules- payment from resident or payment for activities in location in Nepal.

Proceeds from sale of trading stock or cost for it is deemed expensed in Nepal, if disposed trading stock is in Nepal at the point of disposal.

Interest, dividend, governmental employment, retirement payments, annuities, or other investments returns deemed to having in source in Nepal, if paid by a resident of Nepal.

Other income or associated expense to that income deemed to be had source in Nepal based on the location of the payment-base.

For example, right to use or restriction on use for Nepal assets as natural resources, rent, royalty, insurance risk, service rendered, Cross boarder data transmission from equipment installed in Nepal.

Cross boarder transport initiating from Nepal is deemed as source having in Nepal, but it excludes transshipments in Nepal.

Income from any other activities within Nepal is deemed as source in Nepal.

For the source of expense, all the matching cost for income having source in Nepal is deemed as Nepal source expense.

36 **In case, the business suffers loss. Does it allow for set off?**

Business loss allows set off for seven-years in general case and twelve-years in case of power-sector, BOOT or petroleum extraction business. Investments loss is allowed for seven-years.

Unrelieved loss from business after seven-years or twelve-years is not allowed to set off with business profits. These losses may be offset with the gain from disposal of business assets or liability forever.

In case of site-PE created from Internation competitive bidding procedure, carry back of loss is allowed, because, long-term contract income recognition on percentage of completion basis on estimated revenue.

37 **How may a foreign subsidiary be having accumulated tax loss obtains the benefit form merging the company to another subsidiary having profit? Does corporate law allow merger of company controlled by foreigners with the company controlled by Nepali nationals?**

Under the view point of taxation, merger of two or more entities is almost another loss making decision. Carry forward of loss is allowed to new company in any case. Moreover, all assets and liabilities of merging company deemed to be disposed at market price on the date of merger. Merged company cannot obtain any tax attributes and deferrals from merging company.

Merger of companies or entities is not the controlling business of tax law. However, deregistration of merging company is required.

Corporate law has not any restriction on merging domestic controlled company with foreign controlled company. However, a company having special business license need to obtain permission from license regulatory for merger or demerger or other corporate restructuring.

38   **What is the treatment of research and development cost for corporate tax?**

Research and development cost for mining is allowed to capitalize and allows for depreciation. The rate is same as depreciation rate for plant and machineries (same pool of depreciable assets).

Research and development cost other than for mining activities is allowed to the extent of fifty-percent of taxable profit before deduction for research and development cost itself. Remaining cost, if any is allowed to capitalize in the pool of plant and machinery.

39   **How does foreign currency account recognize for taxation? If foreign investor deposited its equity fund into bank account, does the foreign exchange gain is taxable?**

For financial accounts, gain or loss on monetary items of cash, bank deposit, receivables or payables foreign currency accounts need to recomputed on the reporting date.

However, for taxation, only realized gain is income. Foreign currency assets either form of cash or bank deposit or receivables need not convert into year-end rate for taxation.

40   **Does Nepal tax have weighted deduction or acceleration on deduction?**

Deductible expense is on transactional basis only. There is no provision for weighted deduction as additional deduction than actual expenditure.

For the depreciation, there are acceleration rule. Manufacturing industry (except negative-externalities), infrastructure business, power producers, power-transmission business or BOOT obtains one-third acceleration on their depreciation rate. In case of installation of power-producing device, fifty - percent of cost is allowed as acceleration on the year of installation.

41 What is the treatment of bad-debt arising during the course of business? Is the bad-debt arising of insolvency (domestic or foreign) allowed for deduction?

Bad-debt if write off after reasonable steps for collection is allowed for deduction. In practical situation, 'reasonable steps for collection' is a vague term. Most cases, of bad-debt is not deductible due to wording of these terms.

In case of insolvency, of course, the waived amount over the collected is a sum where ' reasonable steps for collection' applies and deductible for tax purpose.

For the domestic insolvency, court decides the insolvency and distribute the proceeds through liquidator. In such case, bad-debt is easily acceptable as deduction.

In the foreign insolvency, if the insolvency procedure has under the supervision of court of respective country, the bad-debt is deductible as well as domestic case. In the voluntary liquidation or personal declaration of insolvency is, practically, not allowed for deduction.

42 What is the impact of liability not required pay after deduction for taxable profit has obtained in earlier year?

Taxpayer requires to claim the deduction of expense in the year of expense based on accrual basis of accounting. Therefore, there are numerous cases of deduction before actual payment to the payee.

In the course of business and further negotiation, the obligation to pay may reduce for various reasons. In such case, the benefit which is the liability not

CORPORATE TAX

requires to pay is income for taxable profits in the year when the liability ceases to obligation to pay.

43 Does Nepal tax have thin-capitalization rule? How does interest to borrowed fund from its shareholders or associated enterprise tackle in corporate tax?

Nepal tax law has not concept of thin–capitalization rule nor formal ceiling for debt-to-equity ratio. The parent company or associated enterprise of parent company of Nepal subsidiary may lend as other lending.

Regarding interest rate or other consideration, the rate and conditions for borrowings must be equivalent to the arm's length price principle. If the rate of interest or other considerations is more favorable than prevailing interest rate, transfer pricing rule applies. If the foreign lender seems not associated enterprise in formal way, the anti-income splitting rule or general anti-avoidance rule applies for unnatural rates.

The interest expense is allowed for deduction of taxable profit of the company. however, there is ceiling to allow deduction in a particular tax-year. The maximum deductible interest, if paid to non-resident will be interest income plus 50% of taxable profit before charging the interest.

44 How does income recognize in case of construction contract for contractors? Does engineering procurement contract (EPC) has special recognition rule?

Contractor of construction contract or supervisors on it requires to recognize income from individual contract on percentage of completion basis on cost to cost comparison of estimated cost. Contract revenue recognition is somewhat similar with the revenue recognition under International Financial Reporting Standards.

Revenue recognition of EPC contract is same as regular construction contracts like designed by employer or other.

In the case of loss from construction contract to the foreign contractor, carry back is allowed.

45 **Does Nepal tax have special treatments for hybrid financial instruments?**

Tax law treats the 'as if' position for hybrid financial instruments like convertibles or preference instruments. In case of convertible bonds, tax law treats it as borrowed fund till its existence of bond. At the point of conversion, market price of converted instrument is deemed as disposal proceeds for bond.

Capital for an entity includes both equity share capital and preference share capital, whether convertible or not. For the case of redeemable preference share capital, capital-first rule applies at the point of redemption.

46 **In case the company fails to pay its corporate tax, what is responsibility of its directors or managers?**

In case an entity fails to pay tax, tax officer may charge the tax to the responsible manager of the company. For this personal liability, tax officer may charge to the existing managers (if they have responsibility to make decision to pay tax) or retired within last six months (again if they have responsibility to make decision to pay tax). The manager, who have evidence to make decision to pay tax (and probably became minority) is not a responsible manager for this purpose.

Once the tax has been paid by the responsible manager personally, s/he can recover it from entity in the question.

Alternatively, taxation authority may, in writing, issue the order of stoppage for seventy-two ours to out of country. This period may be extended by the order of High Court.

Even above two cases of personal liability seem as extreme measure for collection of tax-arrears but has not utilized yet.

47 **Suppose, a foreign enterprise has more than one subsidiary in Nepal either both directly controlled from patent enterprise or one has control over**

other. Does tax law allow to consolidate tax return? Does transfer from one subsidiary to another recognize revenue or is it just group inventory?

For the taxation, company whether parent or subsidiary, each requires to file separate income tax return. No consolidation requires or permits. A group company cannot consolidate the intra-group transfer in single inventory and deferral on recognition is not permitted.

48 How to pay the corporate tax?

Corporate tax is payable in installments. The first installment is minimum of 36% of real annual tax and payable within six-months from beginning of tax-year. The second installment need to reach at least 63% of real annual tax and payable within nine-months from beginning of tax-year. The third installment need to be ninety percent in real annual tax and payable within tax-year. Remaining tax need to pay within three months from end of tax-year.

For delay, there is interest at the rate of 15% p.a. for month and part of month basis.

49 Does the taxpayer certify the tax return itself or need third-party attestation?

Taxpayer requires to certify all the tax return either income tax return, WHT return, VAT return etc. In the online submission, taxpayer requires verification using system code or passkey.

In the case of income return, the taxpayer need to obtain attestation of its tax return from the person having certificate of practice.

50 Does taxpayer need to claim the tax concession or reduced tax benefits or are these automatic benefit?

For any tax benefit, even for eligible deductible expense, taxpayer must claim through its income tax return. Taxpayer need to ensure the full compliance as well as full aware of claiming tax benefits, if any before filing the return, because, taxpayer cannot amend the income tax return after filing to the taxation authority.

51 How to obtain DTA benefit in case of corporate tax?

Corporate tax on taxable profit of a PE is determined as similar as resident domestic company. PE requires to *suo motu* complied with and claimed for DTA benefits, if any. For example, DTA with Mauritius, Pakistan, Qatar, Sri Lanka and Thailand has force of attraction rule. Resident owner of these countries having PE in Nepal need to aggregate the whole transaction of same or similar goods or other activities in Nepal, whether manager of PE has knowledge on it or not. In case of agency-PE, the agent in Nepal may not aware of Nepal transaction of principal enterprise bypassing from his agency. Even in this case, dependent agent is liable to pay tax on behalf of principal enterprise.

Each taxpayer requires to file the transaction details (both purchase and sale) with other parties as well as imports and exports. Taxation authority uses the matching software for these transaction. Mismatch, if any, creates unwanted tax burden, if not at least administrative burden to the taxpayer. It is advisable to taxpayers that reconciliation with each import and export and with each buyers and suppliers during the tax-year.

Taxpayer need to file numerous documents along with income tax return. Many of the taxpayer does not file at the time of filing tax return. When the taxation authority initiates the reassessment (average period almost three years), they cannot produce the require data and reconciliation due to time lapses on the transaction or cannot obtain the supporting from third party. Taxpayer need to avoid this manual hurdle to create unnecessary burden.

Some of the tax concession are time-based concession. For example, particular industry may obtain partial tax concession for specified period, say five- years. After the first-year of benefit, the provision may have repealed from the tax law. Many taxpayer creeps to claim these tax benefit, forgetting the original provision was periodic benefit, and allows to that taxpayer irrespective of the current provision.

CORPORATE TAX

52 **How does a foreign investor assure the stability of taxation provisions? What shall be the impact in case of amendment of tax law unfavorable to the foreign enterprise?**

Taxation provisions are comparable stable for a foreign enterprise because of three major factors.

The first is, the tax law has been drafted with conformity of international standards and best practices usable in developing countries. All of the tax laws are drafted with the close observation from development partners and foreign professionals. Uniformity of the taxation provision within South Asian countries is another benchmarking for tax or trade laws.

The second is, one of the basic principle underlying the tax law is non-discrimination rule between national and foreigners. The tax law confirms same level of taxation to both nationals and foreign person or foreign enterprise. Provisions where same clause is not applicable the suitable provision has maintained with doctrine of horizontal equity.

The third and most important is, if any foreign investor may enter into an agreement with the government for stable tax benefit during its presence in the agreed business in Nepal. Any unfavorable provisions in the amended tax law will not affect the existing tax benefit to that foreign enterprise. Amendments in the tax law in line with favor to the taxpayer is allowed in this case too. This stand-still agreement is allowed for the foreign enterprise in the infrastructure or power sector business only.

53 **Is there any tax based on capital? Does capital investments credit allow for corporate tax?**

Income tax is purely income-based taxation. Nepal does not levy tax on capital. In case of investments in land and building, local governments have property tax system. The amount of tax depends upon the area of land and size of building. The rate is location specific. Federal or provincial or local authority do not allow any investments credits to compute corporate tax or any other taxes.

WITHHOLDING TAX

54 Does Nepal tax has withholding tax?

Nepal tax has withholding tax mechanism. Resident payer need to withhold tax on variety of Nepal-sourced payments of income to domestic payee as well as foreign payee.

The withholding tax is compulsory compliance to the payer. If case, payer fails to withhold tax, it is deemed withholding tax at the time of payment.

Withholding tax is deemed as part of payment to the concern payee. In case, there is deemed withholding tax, therefore, payer can recover from the withholdee are receivable. However, payer cannot recover the fees and interest for delay payments. The fee is 2.5% p.a. for non-filing and 50% of withholding tax for non-reporting. The delay payment interest is 15% p.a. for month and part of a month in all cases of delay payment.

55 Is there any withholding tax to the foreign exparts?

Resident employee or non-resident employee, if the remuneration of employment has paid by a resident entity (subsidiary or PE is resident entity for Nepal tax purpose), they need to withhold the applicable tax on each payment under employment.

WITHHOLDING TAX

An individual residing Nepal for a period of 183 or more days is resident individual. Therefore, employment payment for an individual residing Nepal for less than that period, the withholding tax rate is 25% of gross remuneration (cash or facilities). In such situation, 183-days rule is not applicable, if the payer is resident PE.

In case of resident employee (irrespective of nationality), there is progressive tax rate from 0% to 36%. Resident employer need to withhold tax on equal installment based on estimated annual income from own source to a particular employee.

In case of foreign exparts, the remuneration for the works in Nepal is subject to withholding tax from its employer. If the portion of employee's remuneration is payable in home country, then there are two distinct situations. If the resident entity books these home-country remuneration, withholding is must, otherwise the resident PE or subsidiary fails to report appropriate taxable profits.

56   How to value the cost for residency of foreign exparts working in the Nepal office or sites?

The value of benefit from residency in a building is token value of 2% of monthly salary to that employee. Similar the case with vehicle facility, which is 0.5% of salary paid and payable to the employee.

The valuation is same in case of single or common house either furnished or not. The cost of rent paid by the employer is irrelevant in this case.

In the case of employee, who is not on monthly salary but on assignment basis or on the basis of milestones or otherwise, the value of benefit for residency is deemed to be 25% of rent actually paid his/her employer.

57   How to tax on retirement payments- to domestic employee or exparts?

Any types of retirement payments like gratuity, accumulated leave, or otherwise as per the employment contract is subject to 15% WHT to all employees- domestic or foreign. The WHT in this regard is final. Therefore, retiring employee need not file annual tax return for retirement payment.

58 **Does foreign employee need file annual tax return, even after withholding tax on remuneration?**

Employee being a non-resident having remuneration for resident payer has 25% tax on each payment. Payments subject to withholding tax are final in nature. Therefore, non-resident employee need not file annual tax return.

Resident employee, either national or foreign, need not to file annual tax return, if s/he has only the employment income from single resident employer. Employee having multiple employments or have other income (except final withholding taxed income) requires to file annual tax return. The filing the return is same deadline as corporate tax. In that case, tax withheld by the employer is allowed for credit to annual tax.

59 **Does employer need to file details of employees or payment information to the authority?**

Taxpayer requires to file annual tax return along with many details including employees' remuneration and WHT details. Employee specific details contains name, annual remuneration, withheld tax on those remunerations. Annual payroll computation reconciling total payroll expense in the financial statement with the total payroll expenses in the tax return.

60 **Does personal income tax on non-resident individuals who travel temporarily to the country during the year and perform personal services within country?**

Employment of foreign employee, temporarily travel to employment in Nepal is taxable as non-resident. Non-resident individuals need to include all income earned in Nepal (similar to resident individual) for calculating individual PIT liability.

WITHHOLDING TAX

All the reimbursements by the employer are deemed as part of taxable income of the non-resident individual. In case free accommodation and free vehicle facility is provided to the employee, presumptive value of 2% and 0.5% of salary respectively is deemed to be received by the employee, irrespective of actual expense paid for those facilities. If, however, these facilities are reimbursed in cash, total payment made for the same is added for calculating the taxable base.

61. What are the withholding tax applicable to parent company, or foreign entity?

Resident entity (subsidiary or PE) need to withhold following withholding tax to the non-resident person (foreign person whether parent enterprise, associated enterprise or any other enterprises):

Royalty payment - 15% WHT on gross payment. Royalty or technical fee from the entity operating under Special Economic Zone has WHT at 7.5% of gross payment. All DTAs maximum rate of 15% in all cases, however, India and Norway have most favor nation clause automatically actable whereas Korea and Mauritius has negotiable.

Importation service from aboard – 15% WHT on gross payment.

Contract for supply of goods, construction, repairs – 5% WHT on gross payment.

Bandwidth or radio-wave related payment or transmission of electricity – 10% WHT on gross payment.

Aircraft repairs - – 5% WHT on gross payment.

Dividend from subsidiary – 5% WHT on gross payment.

Interest or similar investments returns – 15% WHT on gross payment.

Withholding tax will not applicable in above case, if paid to parent company, which resident of contracting state having DTA with Nepal.

Withholding requirement to the payment to resident payee has not addressed here.

62 What is the impact of re-characterization of payment to parent company under transfer pricing?

In case any payments against the procurement from associated enterprises is subject to WHT. For example, service from associated enterprise is subject to 15% WHT on gross payment. Similar is the case for interest payments. In case, these transaction has re-characterized under transfer pricing rule, the event create difficult situation of tax for both PE or to its parent company. In this situation, the over-paid amount will be added back with domestic PE for corporate tax. It creates corporate tax, fees equivalent to 100% of corporate tax and interest till date of payment in PE's side. Overpaid amount is deemed as dividend to parent company and need to pay dividend tax along with interest. Legally, withholding tax on service payment or interest payment is refundable, which is practically rare.

CAPITAL GAIN TAX

63. **Does Nepal tax law have capital gain tax system?**

Nepal tax law has capital gain tax mechanism. Legally, capital gain is called as net-gain on disposal of non-business chargeable assets.

When foreign shareholder disposes the securities in Nepal company, the gain is subject to 25% of capital gain tax. The tax rate is similar to both listed securities as well as unlisted securities. Securities for this purpose is both shares in subsidiary or portfolio investments in company or lending instruments.

The rate of tax is 25% of capital gain from disposing shares held by an entity. Method of payment is – 15% through Tax Collection at Source (TCS) from company having shares and 10% through installment and at the time of filing income tax return. Disposing shareholder requires to file income tax return within three months from date of exit from the entity. Taxing the capital gain is deemed as primary taxing right and hence, foreign tax credit is not allowed.

For the listed securities, TCS is 10% and remaining 15% require to pay on installments and through annual tax return.

In case, foreign parent disposes Nepal PE, the gain on disposal of PE is taxable as corporate tax clubbing this gain too.

| 64 | **Does Nepal tax law have capital gain tax on value sifting on issuance further shares?** |

Nepal tax law has not concept of value sifting either direct value sifting or indirect value sifting.

| 65 | **How does capital gain determine?** |

Capital gain (formal name in Nepal tax is net-gain) is the difference of incomings from disposal of securities with outgoings paid on it. This is the general case of direct investments.

In case a shareholder disposes shares in an entity computation of gain will be different between incomings from disposal (and incomings before disposal, if any) with outgoings. Computation of gain will be on transactional basis, however, in case of transfer without consideration or with insufficient consideration (so-called non-market transfer), valuation of incomings will be on market price1 at the time of disposal.

For example, US Inc. – Greece AE. – Malaysia Bhd. – Czech a.s – France SA. – UAE LLP – Nepal Ltd. are subsidiary in order. UAE LLP has direct investments in shares in Nepal Ltd. In case, UAE LLP disposes its shares in Nepal Ltd., the gain, if any, is subject to Nepal tax as capital gain on disposal. This is the case of direct holding of shares in Nepal Ltd. and tax incidence to the gain-making party.

What will happen if France SA. disposes share in UAE LLP? UAE LLP has direct investment in Nepal Ltd. and its owner has changed. Net-worth and business of Nepal Ltd. is one of the base for valuation of shares in UAE LLP. In this case the gain on shares in Nepal Ltd. will be computed and tax is levied on gain, if any. In this case, taxing person is France SA. Tax obligation of Nepal Ltd. has to collect advance tax (15% of gain). Remaining tax (10% of gain) requires to be paid by France SA. itself.

---

[1] Section 45 of Income Tax Act, 2058.

CAPITAL GAIN TAX

Therefore, there is tax incidence from capital gain in the case of direct or indirect disposal of shares in NTC by its shareholders.

66 **How to use DTA benefits for capital gain tax?**

Article 13 of each DTA where Nepal is a contracting state has capital gain provision. Capital gain on disposing shares in Nepal company has limited primary taxing right to source country (Nepal). In such case, treaty provision will apply over taxation law.

In all DTAs, capital gain arising alienation of immovable property situated in Nepal has unlimited primary taxing right in Nepal. Therefore, resident of DTA countries deriving capital gain from alienation of immovable property situated in Nepal is taxable as regular tax payer.

Capital gain as described in DTAs from alienation of movable properties forming part of PE or PE itself is subject to corporate tax clubbing with taxable profits.

In all cases of DTAs, capital gain from the alienation of ships or aircraft operated in international traffic has primary taxing right with the country of resident or effective management. Therefore, Nepal will not tax on these capital gains.

Capital gain on alienation of shares in Nepal company consisting directly or indirectly with substantial portion form immovable property is taxable in Nepal as regular tax payer.

Capital gain on alienation of shares in Nepal company, if the Chinese or Pakistani or Thai shareholder holds 25% or more shares, is taxable in Nepal.

Capital gain on alienation of shares in Nepal company derived by resident of Austria, India, Republic of Korea, Mauritius, Norway, Qatar and Sri Lanka is not taxable in Nepal. Similarly, capital gain on alienation of shares in Nepal company derived by resident holding less than 25% of issued share from China, Pakistan, and Thailand is not taxable in Nepal.

For the alienator, who is subject to tax on capital gain on alienation of said asset requires to pay tax. In case, the alienating asset is company, the company itself requires to make TCS at 15% of gain and remaining 10% of gain requires to pay through installments and annual tax returns. For other cases, the alienator requires to file income tax return for payment of tax.

67 **Is it compulsory to receive proceeds on disposal of shares in Nepal or may be received elsewhere? What is the process to repatriate the sales proceeds from alienation of shares in Nepal company or Nepal PE?**

For the investments channeled through Foreign Investment and Technology Transfer law, disposal of shares from foreign investor need to obtain approval from DOI in the case of exit of foreign investments. In this case, upon DOI's permission central bank allows repatriation of proceeds from disposal of shares. Alternatively, disposal model may be changing the foreign owner but not the exit of foreign investments. In this case, the settlement may be done anywhere within or beyond Nepal. In both cases, Nepal has concern on approved level of FDI, but not the quantum of proceeds.

DIVIDEND TAX AND REPATRIATION TAX

68   **What is the dividend tax based on Nepal tax law?**

Income after corporate tax is distributable to its shareholders. The distribution is allowed as capitalization to securities and payment to shareholders. In both cases, there is dividend tax at 5% of distributed amount (capitalized or paid) levied to the shareholders under final withholding tax mechanism.

In case of payment to shareholders having other business payments, the priority comes in the question. Out of payments, firstly, the portion of liability against the purchases from shareholders is deemed to be paid. Out of remaining amount of payment, second priority goes to distribution to the extent of net-worth valued at market price on the date of payment. The least priority is deemed as capital refund.

Sometimes, the payment triggers four level of priorities. For example, parent company has investments in shares in subsidiary, has interest bearing fund, has receivables from sales and potential dividend from subsidiary. In such situation, the payment to shareholder has priorities as – payment of receivables from sales, interest bearing instruments, distribution to the extent of net-worth at market price and capital refund.

There is one exception in general rule of profit-first rule. In case the payment to shareholder based on buy-back of shares from subsidiary, then capital-first rule applies. In this case, the amount of capital reduction (in formal way) is deemed to be had paid first and remaining amount is deemed as dividend.

For a PE, amount paid to its parent company as well as to other associated enterprises are tested exactly same as above. The amount equivalent to distribution from that calculation is subject to repatriation tax at 5%. One point is different in repatriation tax than distribution tax is, repatriation tax is levied to PE itself, not to the parent company. This makes repatriation tax is effectively higher than distribution tax.

69 Is dividend tax waived or reduced?

In case of industries established in Special Economic Zone, there is periodic waiver and reduced rate of 2.5% of dividend tax. Similarly, in case, manufacturing or tourism industry capitalize its profits to increase the installed capacity, the capitalization is dividend tax free.

For the company which derives the dividend income, corporate tax is waived for portion of income comprised from dividend income. If such company distributes the dividend further to its shareholder, no dividend tax is levied to the extent of dividend income accrued till that days.

Similar provision is applicable to the PE too. PE deriving dividend income need not to pay corporate tax on this dividend income.

70 Does corporate tax paid by entity allowed for imputation on tax on dividend?

Company pays corporate tax on taxable profits. Tax paid income of company allows for distribution of dividend. On the distribution of dividend, dividend tax is levied at 5% under withholding procedure. Based on tax to the company and shareholder on the same income, there is economic double taxation.

DIVIDEND TAX AND REPATRIATION TAX

If the company earns the income from dividend, this is not taxable income for corporate profit. At the point of distribution, no dividend tax is levied on the distribution to the extent of dividend income included in profit. Therefore, dividend income of a company as well as redistribution has no tax. To this extent, imputation facility embedded in tax law.

Similarly, in case of repatriation of income from PE, there is double taxation.

However, in both cases of dividend tax or repatriation tax, the rate is token rate of 5%.

71. **Are there any formalities to repatriate dividend from Nepal subsidiary of Nepal PE?**

For the repatriation of dividend declared from a company in Nepal or a PE having tax paid income, the permission to repatriation is required. The process to obtain permission to repatriate is simple with few regular documentations. The required documents are as dividend payment formalities (annual general meeting resolution), tax filing certificate on these dividends and corporate tax, regulatory approval, if licensed business, request letter from concern company.

In case of repatriation of profits from a PE, similar documentation like tax payment, tax filing certificate, is required. None cases, written approval from the taxation authority is required document for repatriation.

TAX DEADLINES

72 **What are the tax deadlines during business operation in Nepal?**

Registration in taxation authority is required initiation of business actives during preparatory period. VAT registration along with income tax registration is beneficial due to input tax credit associated on preparatory actives and capital assets. However, VAT registration is permissible within thirty-days from date of crossing of threshold for compulsory registration.

Once registered in VAT, monthly VAT return requires to file within twenty-five days from closure of tax-period (Nepali calendar month). VAT return is compulsory even the cases when no transaction occurs (zero-return). Non-filers are subject to penalty. There is no annual VAT return.

Within first month of new tax-year, certified copy of VAT purchase book and VAT sales book requires to certified from tax officer.

For withholding tax, taxpayer requires to file monthly WHT return within twenty-five days from closure of tax-period (Nepali calendar month). In case, the month has not any WHT, filing a zero-return is not required.

TAX DEADLINES

For tax collected at source (TCS) on capital gain, taxpayer requires to file monthly TCS return within twenty-five days from closure of tax-period (Nepali calendar month). In case, the month has not any TCS, filing a zero-return is not required.

For income tax, estimated tax return is required within six-months from beginning of tax-year.

Taxpayer requires to file its annual income tax return within three months from end of tax-year. Upon written application with valid reasons, taxation authority may extend this deadline for further three-months at once or from time to time.

73 **What are the deadlines for the information or other documents apart from regular returns?**

In case, taxation authority instructs for any information or data or document, in writing, taxpayers requires to submit the required data, information or documents within fifteen-days from date of receipt of such notices.

In case of changes in substance of information provided during registration, the changes require to inform in writing within fifteen-days from those changes. Failure to submit these documents and information have both fee for non-compliance and fine as offence.

During the reassessment, the taxation authority seeks clarification on proposed reassessment. Taxpayer requires to reply along with further evidences within fifteen-days (for jeopardy-assessment this period is seven-days) from date of receipt of those proposed reassessments. Failure to respond this has not any fee or fine.

74 **What are the appeal deadline on tax disputes?**

Taxpayer who is not satisfy the decision of tax officer may file its administrative appeal to the Director General of Inland Revenue Department (DG) within thirty-days from date of receipt of those decision. This thirty-days may be extendable by Director General if taxpayer applies within seven-days from end of first thirty-days with valid reasons for extension.

General period for decision on administrative review is sixty-days from date of appeal. After sixty-days, if DG does not decide yet, taxpayer may lodge a letter to DG to apply own appeal grievances with revenue tribunal.

Taxpayer requires to file an appeal to revenue tribunal within thirty-five days from the date of receipt of decision from DG or from date of letter to DG. These thirty-five days may be extendable further thirty-days if taxpayer applies within thirty-days from end of thirty-five days with valid reasons for extension.

75 **What is the deadline for personal rulings?**

Taxpayer may request for personal ruling (legally called as advance-ruling) on the matter of clarification on the provision applicable to own business. Taxation authority may respond the ruling request within forty-five days from date of request lodge. If the authority did not respond the request, the request deemed to be decided unfavorable to the taxpayer. After lapse of said forty-five days, the taxpayer may file an application of appeal against said unfavorable decision.

76 **Can a taxpayer amend filed tax returns and documents?**

Taxpayer can amend Estimated tax return, practically worthless.

Taxpayer may amend or add the documents submitted to the authority.

Income tax return, VAT return, WHT or TCS return cannot be amended after filing with the authority.

77 **What are the payment deadlines for Nepal tax?**

For registration, there is not any payment of tax. Tax officer may decide for the security deposit from Foreign PE, but this is refundable deposit.

VAT, WHT and TCS requires to pay within twenty-five days from closure of respective collection month.

Installment tax requires to pay within six-months of tax-year (36% of real tax), within next three-months (27% of real tax) and to the end of tax-year (27% of real tax).

TAX DEADLINES

Remaining annual tax (10% of real tax) requires to pay within three-months from end of tax-year. WHT, if any is adjustable into installment tax.

For the purpose of installment tax and annual tax, real tax means the sum of corporate tax on taxable profit and repatriation tax from PE.

Reassessed tax by tax officer requires to pay within prescribed timeframe on reassessment order, which is normally fifteen-days from receipt of reassessment notice.

Payment deadlines are strict and extension is not permitted in any case. Failure to pay within prescribed time creates interest at 15% p.a. for month and part of month basis.

TAX SPARING BENEFIT

78 **Does Nepal tax have special concessional tax system? Does foreign investors from the countries having tax treaty with Nepal obtains tax sparing benefits for those concession tax or exemption?**

Nepal tax has various types of tax concessions. Most of them are in manufacturing industry creating employment (some cases restricted to creating national employment), tourism industry, infrastructure industry with or without BOOT, hydropower or alternative power sector and information technology. The tax concession is allowed to the person fulfilling the condition of concession irrespective of jurisdiction of ownership. Both PEs or foreign subsidiaries in Nepal obtains the tax concession benefits.

For the taxpayer from non-DTA countries, the concession from Nepal tax will have no attraction, because corporate tax itself is comparably low in Nepal comparing capital exporting countries. However, residents from DTA countries may obtain tax benefits to the corporate level, if the tax treaty has tax-sparing clause on it. From the following list of tax-sparing provision, resident of Norway had limited tax-sparing benefit for limited period of ten-year, which has lapsed in 2007.

Nepal has tax-sparing provisions in the following DTAs:

TAX SPARING BENEFIT

Nepal-Austria DTA, Art. 22 – Para. 4. For the purpose of allowance as credit in a Contracting State, the tax paid in the other Contracting State shall be deemed to include the tax which is otherwise payable in that other State but has been reduced or waived by that State under its legal provisions for tax incentives.

Nepal-China DTA, Art. 23 - Para. 3. For the purpose of allowance as credit in a Contracting State, the tax paid in the other Contracting State shall be deemed to include the tax which is otherwise payable in that other State but has been reduced or waived by that State under its legal provisions for tax incentives.

Nepal-Korea (Republic of) DTA, Art. 23 - Para. 1 (b) Notwithstanding the provisions of sub-paragraph a), there shall be deemed to have been paid by the Korean resident the amount which would have been paid as Nepal tax under the laws of Nepal and in accordance with this Agreement if the Nepal tax had not been reduced or exempted in Nepal in accordance to any special incentive measures designed to promote economic development in Nepal, which are effective on the date of signature of this Agreement or which may be introduced in the future in laws relating to Nepal tax in place of, or in addition to, the existing measures, provided that an agreement is made between the Governments of the two Contracting States in respect of the scope of the benefit accorded to the taxpayer by the said measures.

Nepal-Mauritius DTA, Art. 23 - Para. 3. For the purposes of allowance as a credit the tax payable in Mauritius or Nepal as the context requires, shall be deemed to include the tax which is otherwise payable in either of the two Contracting States but has been reduced or waived by either State in order to promote its economic development.

Nepal-Norway DTA, Art. 23 - Para. 1(c) Where exemption from or reduction of Nepalese tax, payable in accordance with the provisions of Article 7 in respect of profits derived by a Norwegian enterprise from a permanent establishment situated in Nepal, has been granted under Nepalese law designed to extend time limited tax incentive to promote foreign investment for the purpose of the economic development of Nepal, then, for the purposes of subparagraph a) (i) deduction from Norwegian tax for Nepalese tax shall be allowed as if no such exemption or reduction had been granted, provided that the permanent establishment is engaged in business activities (other than business activities in the financial sector) and that no more than 25 percent of such profits consist of interest and gains from the alienation of shares or bonds, or consist of profits derived from third states.

Nepal-Pakistan DTA, Art. 22 - Para. 3. A grant given by a Contracting State or a political subdivision thereof to a resident of the other Contracting State in accordance with laws designed to promote economic development in that first-mentioned State, shall not be taxable in the other State.

Nepal-Qatar DTA, Art. 23 - Para. 2. For the purpose of allowance as credit as the case may be, in a Contracting State, the tax paid in the other Contracting State shall be deemed to include the tax which is otherwise payable in that other State but has been reduced or waived by that State under its legal provisions for tax incentives.

Nepal – Sri Lanka DTA, Art. 23 - Para. For the purpose of allowance as a credit in a Contracting State, the tax paid in the other, Contracting State shall be deemed to include the tax which is otherwise payable in that other State but has been reduced or waived by that State under its legal provisions for tax incentives.

Nepal-Thailand DTA, Art. 23 - Para. 4. For the purpose of allowance as a credit in a Contracting State, the tax paid in the other, Contracting State shall be deemed to include the tax which is otherwise payable in that other State but has been reduced or waived by that State under its legal provisions for tax incentives.

The tax sparing provision with Norway has limited scope for the first 10 years for which the Agreement is effective. The competent authorities shall consult each other in order to determine whether this period shall be extended. Further negotiation and extension of sparing period has not concluded yet.

TAX SPARING BENEFIT

79 **What are the waivers and concession those may trigger to be beneficial to resident of DTA countries?**

Following are the examples of tax waiver or tax concessions as on end of 2018, may be beneficial to the resident of contracting states as above.

Manufacturing industry excluding manufacturing of negative externalities and information technology industry obtains concession of 10% to 30% of corporate based on the number of Nepali employees (100 to more than 500), further 10% concession if employment composition has more than one-third from female or incapacitated person. This makes effective tax rate for 2018 from 14% to 18% of taxable profit for manufacturing industry and 17.5% to 22.5% for IT industry.

Manufacturing industry excluding manufacturing of negative externalities obtains concession of 70% to 90% of corporate tax for the first ten years, based on remoteness of the factory. This makes effective tax rate for 2018 from 14% to 18% of taxable profit.

Manufacturing industry excluding manufacturing of negative externalities having capital employed US$ 10 million or more obtains concession of 100% for the first five-years and 50% of corporate tax for three-years, if it creates direct employment of 500 people. The corporate tax rate before any concession in these business in 20% for 2018.

Manufacturing industry including manufacturing of negative externalities in special economic zone obtains concession of 100% for the first ten years (or seven years for non-remote) and 50% of corporate tax then-after. Foreign royalty is taxed at 50% of actual rate (i.e. 7.5% for 2018), dividend tax is waived for first five-years and levies at 50% of dividend tax rate then-after. The corporate tax rate before any concession in these business in 20% for 2018.

Extraction of petroleum or operation of mine or ore till mid-April 2024, will have 100% waiver in corporate tax for first seven-years and 50% waiver for second three-years. The corporate tax rate before any concession in these business in 20% for 2018.

Cyber related business in specified place obtains 50% of waiver in corporate tax forever. The corporate tax rate before any concession in these business in 25% for 2018.

Exporting of manufacturing goods obtains 25% of waiver in corporate tax. The corporate tax rate before any concession in these business in 20% for 2018.

Roads, bridge, airport, tunnel construction and operation or trolley bus or tram operation obtains 40% of corporate tax waiver. The corporate tax rate before any concession in these business in 20% for 2018.

Tourism industry having capital employed US$ 20 million or more obtains concession of 100% for the first five-years and 50% of corporate tax for three-years. The corporate tax rate before any concession in these business in 25% for 2018.

Tea industry, dairy industry, cloth industry obtains 50% tax waiver in corporate tax. The corporate tax rate before any concession in these business in 20% for 2018.

Above tax concessions are equally available to all foreign enterprise having source in Nepal irrespective of DTA.

If a person obtains more than one options in tax concession, only one option, as opted by the taxpayer is allowed.

FORECE OF ATTRACTION RULE

80 **Does Nepal tax law has force of attraction rule for similar business from parent company of a PE?**

Taxation of PE owned by a foreign resident is taxable in Nepal in accordance with the provision of tax law, if not modified from a tax treaty. Foreign enterprise may have presence in Nepal through a PE. In the same time foreign enterprise may enter into independent business transaction with other parties in Nepal which would be similar with the business of PE too. In such situation, question of taxation raised as how to tax the PE – taxing only on the transactions of the PE itself or taxing the PE with whole of the transactions either from PE or from its head office. Determination of taxable profit of a PE on whole of the income either from PE itself or from head office is force of attraction rule.

Nepal tax law is silent on this regards.

81 **Is there a "connected project" or "connected business" concept for PE purposes in Nepal tax law, such that other business activities in-country could create or enhance PE risk?**

Connected project or connected business creates PE for corporate tax. If a foreign enterprise has more than one business activities connected each other or services in more than one place, it triggers a PE and corporate tax. However, if the projects are independent to each other, they may create a PE individually but not collectively.

82 Does Nepal enter into a tax-treaty having force of attraction rule for similar business from parent company of a PE?

Based on tax treaties with five contracting states, they have force of attraction rule. The excerpt of individual DTA is as follows:

Nepal-Mauritius DTA has FoA clause for same or similar goods or other activities (construction, consulting, services or other) as per "Art. 7, Para. 1 (b) sales in that other State of goods or merchandise of the same or similar kind as those sold through that permanent establishment; or (c) other business activities carried on in that other State of the same or similar kind as those effected through that permanent establishment."

Nepal-Pakistan DTA has FoA clause for same or similar goods or other activities (construction, consulting, services or other) as per "Art. 7, Para. 1 (b) sales in that other State of goods or merchandise of the same or similar kind as those sold through that permanent establishment; or (c) other business activities carried on in that other State of the same or similar kind as those effected through that permanent establishment."

Nepal-Qatar DTA has FoA clause for same or similar goods or other activities (construction, consulting, services or other) as per "Art. 7, Para. 1 (b) sales in that other State of goods or merchandise of the same or similar kind as those sold through that permanent establishment; or (c) other business activities carried on in that other State of the same or similar kind as those affected through that permanent establishment."

Nepal-Sri Lanka DTA has FoA clause for same or similar goods or other activities (construction, consulting, services or other) as per "Art. 7, Para. 1 (b) sales in that other State of goods or merchandise of the same or similar kind as those sold through that permanent establishment; or (c) other business activities

FORECE OF ATTRACTION RULE

carried on in that other State of the same or similar kind as those effected through that permanent establishment."

Nepal-Thailand DTA has FoA clause for same or similar goods or other activities (construction, consulting, services or other) as per "Art. 7, Para. 1 (b) sales in that other State of goods or merchandise of the same or similar kind as those sold through that permanent establishment; or (c) other business activities carried on in that other State of the same or similar kind as those effected through that permanent establishment."

83 **Who is responsible for aggregating transaction based on force of attraction rule applicable for Nepal PE?**

PE requires to *suo motu* complied with and claimed for DTA benefits, if any. DTA with Mauritius, Pakistan, Qatar, Sri Lanka and Thailand has force of attraction rule. Resident owner of these countries having PE in Nepal need to aggregate the whole transaction of same or similar goods or other activities in Nepal, whether manager of PE has knowledge on it or not. In case of agency-PE, the agent in Nepal may not aware of Nepal transaction of principal enterprise bypassing from his agency. Even in this case, dependent agent is liable to pay tax on behalf of principal enterprise. Similar case may arise on a service-PE or site-PE. The manager of services and construction site may or may not aware of the similar transactions from head office. However, it is the responsibility of head office to make aware its manager working in Nepal. In the other side, the manager working in Nepal, need to be aware on the treaty provisions.

CHANGE IN CONTROL

84 What is change in control as per Nepal tax? How does it important for a foreign investor attaching Nepal?

When the control (50% or more) of an entity (company, joint venture, partnership or PE) changes with respect to the controlling structure of last three years, then event is said as change in control.

In case any of the above controller exit from the shareholders of the entity in question, there is tax incidence to the entity itself. The buyer shareholder (as well as seller shareholder) requires to pay a good attention of this tax impact to the entity during their negotiation.

Not only the change in control to the company in the question, but also the change in control in the parent company (or parent(s) of parent company and so on; including foreign parent company) affect the tax attributes in the resident company. For example: say US Inc. – Greece AE. – Malaysia Bhd. – Czech a.s – France SA. – UAE LLP – Nepal Ltd. are subsidiary in order. Change in control in any of above makes impact on Nepal Ltd. change in control measures the real controller, not only the formal controller as pass-through approach. In this example, real shareholders of US Inc. are the real owner of Nepal Ltd. and UAE LLP is just the formal owner. Change in control provision looks to the

CHANGE IN CONTROL

shareholders of US Inc. In case, Grece AE disposes shares in Malaysia Bhd., the ultimate owner of Nepal Ltd. will transfer from shareholders of US Inc. to shareholders of buyer company. That means Nepal Ltd. handled by new set up of shareholders under pass-through approach.

Therefore, either direct change in control or indirect change in interposed owners, change in control provision will apply.

Potential question of non-discrimination has better to address in this case. Above example has taken to exhibit the effect to the foreign investors. In the case of domestic chain (i.e. assume all the above companies are resident companies and underlying shareholders are Nepali) as in above example, the outcome is same.

Tax impact of change in control is simple. All the assets and liabilities of company (in this example Nepal Ltd.) deemed to be disposed at market price to new-controlled company (again to Nepal Ltd as self-supply at market price). Any gain on those deemed transfer is subject to corporate tax. None of the tax deferrals is allowed to carried forward to new-control company, hence, tax loss, if any, cannot be transferred into new-controlled company.

The outgoing shareholders require to pay tax on capital gain on shares valued based on underlying assets of company. In the same time company itself requires to pay tax on unrealized gain from own assets. Both the buyer and seller shareholder pay a good attention in this provision of tax before making any share purchase agreements. To mitigate this parallel taxation, better way to valuation of shares using gross-down method.

85 **How to determine the change in control in case changes were not fifty percent or more at a time?**

Determination of change in control has three major points.

Firstly, only the changes in shareholders having one percent or more (and associated person holder less than it) is basis to evaluation the change.

Secondly, the changes will compare with the shareholding pattern of three years earlier date. This method accommodates all the changes even without changes in controlling shareholders.

Thirdly, entry of new shareholders is deemed as change, because there is zero control in the date which is three years earlier than date of entry.

Therefore, change in control triggers by changing portfolio shareholders too. It is not required to change in shareholders of controlling shareholders.

86 **How to value the assets and liabilities on the date of change in control?**

Valuation of business or assets and liability is a controversial matter in the Nepali business environment. It is still unclear that whether above market price includes fair value of business or fair value of assets only. Company owning land and using restricted free-hold properties is another critical item for valuation at market price. Company is required to pay tax on unrealized gain.

In case of change in control of 100% shares, valuation will be more easy than changes in small proportion. Almost cases, the valuation will be made on asset-to-asset basis. However, there are examples of valuation of the business as a whole taking valuation of asset-to-asset and valuation of internal goodwill.

VALUE ADDED TAX

87 **Does Nepal have value added tax? How does VAT works?**

Value Added Tax (VAT) is indirect tax applicable for supply of goods or services within Nepal, import into Nepal or export from Nepal.

The rate is single rate of 13%. Supplier collects VAT at 13% of its each and every supply of goods or services. There are numerus exempt items mainly on goods of basic needs.

Export of goods obtains zero-rate facility of VAT. Export of service, if consumed outside Nepal obtains zero-rate facility.

Small vendors apply for registration when their transaction crosses the compulsory registration thresholds. However, almost business enterprises register themselves voluntarily.

Customs offices collects VAT on taxable amount of goods imported.

Only the registered person may collect VAT. The collection date or deemed collection date is the earliest of date of invoicing, delivery of goods or services or payment of consideration.

Registered person requires to issue tax invoice in each and every supply. The format of tax invoice has prescribed by regulation. Tax invoice must be in sequential order, pre-printed and pre-numbered. Supplier need to produce tax invoice of triplicate basis (for abbreviated tax invoice for retailers duplicate basis). The collected tax (output tax) during the month must reported in VAT return.

Registered person requires to file VAT return monthly on its output tax less input tax basis. Any VAT over input tax need to pay within twenty-five days from closure of month of collection. For the delay payment, interest at 15% p.a. and additional duty at 10% p.a. on arrears on the monthly basis.

88 **What is supply for the purpose of VAT?**

VAT is levied on 'taxable supply' of goods and services. The term 'taxable Supplies' refers to supplies of goods and services completed by a registered person for 'consideration' in the course of, or as a part of the person's business activities and includes:

i. The sale, supply or delivery of taxable goods to another person, including imports.

ii. The sale or provision of taxable services to another person.

iii. The appropriation of taxable goods for personal use or for use by others.

iv. The making of a gift of any taxable goods or taxable service in the course of business.

v. The letting of goods on hire, leasing or other transfers.

vi. The processing of data or supply of information or similar service.

vii. The supply of labor or other service.

viii. The export of goods or goods sale or use in international flights.

VALUE ADDED TAX

89   **How does consideration measure on supply for VAT?**

VAT is levied on taxable amount of supply. Taxable amount is consideration plus any transactional-basis taxes and duties. VAT has not cascading effect on itself, therefore, no VAT on VAT levies. However, there are numerous items of supply are exempt for VAT and small vendor need not to register in VAT. Any input crossing through exempt or small vendor chain create VAT cascading.

For the barter or non-cash transaction, valuation will be on market price. Any non-market supply or partial consideration or non-consideration case, the valuation will be on market price.

In fact, all the valuation reached to market price for VAT.

Normal trade discount or quantity discount is allowed for adjustment in taxable amount of supply.

90   **Can government instruct to taxpayer for pricing of supply?**

Government cannot instruct for taxpayer to fixed any price of supply. The overall market is open market for pricing and sales. Taxpayer itself fixes the price of sales but requires publication for the notified goods cases.

If supplier avoids tax through under-invoicing mechanism, taxation authority has right to purchase the remaining stock at under-invoiced priced.

91   **How does input tax allow for offset?**

All the VAT paid on the purchase of goods and services for business including for capital cost is deductible with minimum testing criteria. To obtain input tax credit, purchase tax invoice must contain the name and PAN of the buyer, the purchase must for business having VAT attractive output. VAT paid on personal consumption of food, drinks, entertainment and petrol (mild spirit only, high speed diesel is allowed) for fuel are no-credit items. In case of VAT paid on purchase of light vehicles, only 40% is allowed for input tax credit.

VAT paid on imports and reversed – VAT paid on importation of services is allowed for input tax credit.

The buyer may claim input tax credit within twelve-months from the date of purchase.

92 How to file VAT return and when?

Tax-period for VAT is Nepali calendar month. Taxpayer requires to file VAT return within twenty-five days from end of tax-period. In the return, output tax must be reported in full amount, however, credit may be claimed within twelve-months form date of purchase.

Taxpayer cannot amend the filed return. In case of changes in the reported output tax or input tax through credit note or debit note, the difference may be adjusted in the VAT return after the receipt of or issuance of credit note or debit note accordingly.

93 What is the impact of input tax more than output tax?

If the taxpayer has input tax more than output tax, the net credit amount is carried to the next tax-period. After continuous credit for six-months, taxpayer may apply for refund. Taxpayer having export more than 40% of total sales during tax-period, may apply for immediate refund.

The tax officer refunds the credit within thirty-days in case of export or within sixty-days for six-months credit.

94 What is procedure for assessment of VAT return by tax officer?

Tax officer may examine and assess the VAT within four-years from date of filing of VAT return. During the assessment, tax officer allows the opportunity of hearing issuing preliminary assessment notice. The taxpayer requires to reply the preliminary assessment notice within fifteen-days from date of receipt of such notice.

VALUE ADDED TAX

Apart from regular assessment, tax officer has access and inspection right or examination of records during the tax-period too. In the cases of abuse or potential abuse, tax officer may arrest the taxpayer or may instruct to deposit the security amount as stated in instruction order.

TAX ADMINISTRATION

95 **What the administrative system of taxation authority?**

Inland Revenue Department is responsible federal governmental organization for administration of taxation – income tax, value added tax and excise duty. Department of Customs is responsible for administration of customs. Both of the departments are part of federal ministry of finance. For the taxation matters, Inland Revenue Department has full autonomy in its affairs.

For the extended administration, department has Large Taxpayers' Office (LTO), Medium Taxpayers' Office, Inland Revenue Office and Taxpayers' Service Office.

For the administration of income tax, all the power has vested with the Director General (DG). DG delegates the power to subordinate officers.

For the administrative of value added tax, tax officer has most of the operating power including assessment. DG has policy level powers.

Most of the foreign investors falls under the jurisdiction of LTO. LTO has the policy to review and assess all the taxpayers under its jurisdiction.

Each of offices have the functional section based on its services as tax payer service, tax audit, tax investigation, recovery, documentation and administration.

TAX ADMINISTRATION

96 **How does the local taxation apply for the business owned by foreign investors?**

Nepal is federal country having three levels of governments. Federal government charges the income tax, value added tax, excise duty and customs duty.

Provincial government or local authority has not right to tax on business income.

All the three level of governments are autonomous on the matter of legislature as well as governance. All three level are elected body from the people.

Provincial governments may enact certain taxes based on its own legislature. However, none of the provincial governments enacted any tax laws. Provincial government has not any office set up for tax matters yet.

Local government may enact taxation law regarding business taxation and other taxes. Local government may levy business tax, but it is a small amount of registration and renewals on presumptive tax method. Local government does not charge the tax based on income or profit (exception of few investment income). Local authority charges duties on property.

Local government has simple set of office as a revenue section or revenue division within local authority.

Foreign business set up having multiple outlets within different local authority, sum of presumptive tax payable may become a sizable amount, but still not comparable to the amount of income tax or VAT.

97 **What are the eligible of filing a legal case against the decision of tax officer allow to a taxpayer?**

Apart from extra-ordinary jurisdiction of the courts, following are the area of activities of taxation authority, where an aggrieved taxpayer may file a legal case:

i. Ruling issued from the authority.

ii. Assessment orders for estimated profit for installment, taxable profits for corporate tax, jeopardy assessment, WHT or TCS.

iii. Non-extension for filing income tax return.

iv. Notification to debtor, agent, receivers against notification of paying third-party taxes.

v. Decision against refund of taxes or refusal.

Legal appeal initiated from application for administrative review to the Director General. Against his/her decision appeal to revenue tribunal is allowed.

98 Does Nepal tax allow any types of alternative dispute settlement like arbitration for tax-disputes?

For the tax-disputes, only one mechanism for settlement is administrative review and then revenue tribunal. Administrative review is the quasi-judicial activity of the Director General and revenue tribunal is judicial in nature. Chairperson of the tribunal will be High Court judge or persona having similar qualification and independent. Two other members will come from revenue officer and account office of the government. The question of fact will be final in the decision of revenue tribunal.

Supreme Court may permit the appeal in the case of question of law or minimum compliance of compulsory procedural law or for the question of jurisdiction of the tribunal.

The DTAs have provision regarding mutual agreement procedure; however, the organizational structure of the department nor legal set up has prescribed any clauses for such negotiation.

Nepal has not legal structure of adjudication or arbitration for tax-disputes.

99 How does the authority service the notices to foreign enterprise? Is postal or electronic service obtaining legal validity of servicing notices?

For taxation and corporate law, servicing of notices from governmental offices accepts all means of servicing like hand-over to concern person, delivery into registered office, servicing through pre-stamped post, or publication in newspapers having wide circulation. There may be digital servicing like email or other coded transmissions.

Oral information or short massage from cell phones is not acceptable as servicing of documents.

For the legal activities of taxation, servicing of letter or electronic submission are acceptable.

100 **Does the taxation authority issues rulings for the clarification or misunderstandings?**

For the interpretation of particular provision of the law taxation authority uses two distinct model of ruling. First one is clarification of the issues for all of the taxpayers irrespective of current need or future need. Such clarification is called a public circular. The department is bound to allow the benefit of public circular even if it found contradict with the legal provision.

Second is personal rulings. The taxpayer who is unclear in any provision relating to its transaction may file an application in writing to the Director General. Director General may issue the clarification in writing to that particular taxpayer on the matte of confusion. The department is bound to allow the benefit of such personal ruling until its withdrawn in writing even if it found contradict with the legal provisions.

WORD INDEX

183-days rule
for a PE, **8**, **11**
for residency, **5**, **36**

advance pricing agreement
for transfer pricing, **21**
royalty approval is similar, **21**
same as safe-harbor rule, **21**

annual general meeting
filing corporate return, **3**
for dividend formalities, **46**

arm's length price
for borrowing cost, **30**
method to determine, **21**
on transfer pricing, **19–24**
separate entity concept, **22**
transaction between associated enterprise, **10**

bad-debt

deductible expense, **29**
international insolvency, **29**

BOOT and power-sector
accelerated depreciation, **29**
additional depreciation than accelerated, **26**
additional tax benefit than reduced rate, **26**
loss carry forward period up to twelve-years, **27**
tax-sparing benefit, **51–55**

business loss
carry forward, **27**
carry-back - construction contract, **31**
non-transferable – change in control, **60**
set off, **27**

capital-first rule

71

WORD INDEX

at the point of redemption, 31
on buy-back of shares, 45

chain-of-subsidiary
domestic, 60
of companies, 15
tax treatment for different routes, 14

change in control
definition of, 59
determination of, 60
direct or indirect change, 59
impact in corporate tax, 60
pass-through approach, 59
quantification method, 61

conduit entity
is not allow the DTA benefits, 14

dependent agent
criteria for, 9
in case of force of attraction, 58
is a PE, 7, 8
is liable for tax, 33
no timeframe for a PE, 8

DTA benefits
for capital gain tax, 42
force of attraction rule, 58
is not automatic, 33

force of attraction rule
applicability, 56–58
cases of, 10, 12, 33
definition of, 56
not applicable to a subsidiary, 12
responsibility to compliance, 58

foreign currency accounts
realization basis recognition, 28

General Anti-Avoidance Rule
formal compliance of law, 23
in tax law, 23
income splitting rule, 23

hybrid financial instruments
no special quantification rule, 31

input tax on VAT
conditions to obtain, 64
for capital cost, 17
for preparatory works, 17, 47
over than output tax, 63, 65
partial, 64
reversal through credit note, 65
timing to claim, 65

joint venture
is tax company, 13, 59
of foreign enterprise, 13

language of document, 3, 4

permanent establishment
as per Nepal tax, 7
force of attraction on Nepal DTAs, 56–58
tax sparing provision in Nepal DTAs, 51–55
transfer pricing rule, 19–24

personal rulings
appeal against ruling, 49, 68
deadline to issue, 49
effect till withdrawn, 70

method, 70

research and development cost
capitalization rule, 28
deductible to ceiling of profit, 28

responsible manager
is liable to tax, 31
may issue order of stoppage, 31

service-PE
for force of attraction, 58
minimum timeframe for, 8
of associated enterprises, 13
of parent company, 13
timeframe from DTAs, 11

source of income
for income, 26
legitimacy, 6

tax concessions
current examples, 54
single benefit at a time, 55
to all taxpayer, 51

tax residency
entity, 5
individual, 5

tax sparing
cases of Nepal tax, 51–55
limited and expired with Norway, 53

tax-year
deduction rule, 9, 25
document retaintion period, 10
for 183-days rule, 5
is Nepali calendar year, 4

thin–capitalization rule
no debt-equity ratio, 30
not in tax law, 30

weighted deduction
not applicable for taxation, 28

zero-return
not requires for TCS, 48
not requires for WHT, 47
requires for OCR, 3
requires for VAT, 47

ABOUT THE AUTHOR

CA. Bhava Nath Dahal is an author in Nepal taxation affairs and tax lecturer in leading business school in Nepal. He has involved as tax expert in national tax policy issues and drafting tax code. He is Lead Tax Consultant to Nepal Tax Online. He has served various foreign investors as Lead Tax Consultant Professional Studies Resources Developers Pvt. Ltd.

www.ingramcontent.com/pod-product-compliance
Lightning Source LLC
Chambersburg PA
CBHW071419220526
45469CB00004B/1348